The Promenade

Nishtha Kumar

First published in 2019 by

Becomeshakespeare.com

Wordit Content Design & Editing Services Pvt Ltd
Unit - 26, Building A -1, Nr Wadala RTO,
Wadala (East), Mumbai 400037, India
T: +91 8080226699

Wordit Art Fund helps deserving authors publish
their work by providing monetary support.
To apply for funding, please visit us at
www.BecomeShakespeare.com

ISBN - 978-93-88930-63-5

About the Author

 Nishtha, 24, searched for herself In lacunas within her Only to find remnants of others Cloaked within her flesh She wrote and wrote and wrote Of women & men who caught her fancy Poems and fables of people and places Who can never know what they got into She is a capturer of spirits who doesn't put them shackles She instead, frees them with her words.

Acknowledgment -

This is my first book ever and I want to use this rare opportunity to thank my mother. She lived a short and discontented life due to her illness, but had some lively dreams. She dedicated those dreams to us, my brother and I. She was aware of the fact that she wouldn't be around, to watch us grow become fuller humans but she had a clear idea of what we'll become. She knew she nurtured artists in her house. Although she emphasized on our academics during the daylight, she whispered poetry in our ears by night. She cast this inescapable spell on me with her poems and stories that it shaped my entire existence.

But shaping is not enough, every writer too needs to be watered to grow beyond its pot. To have roots spread across lands. My other mothers did that for me. May we be them, may we raise them sounds banal. We have grown out of this platitude, but somewhere, for me, it lies true.

I have plenty of people to thank, all my lovely friends who forged a supportive team, but maybe next time. This book belongs to all my mother's solely.

The Guiding Light

Contents

What not to do...

You go back home. Lie on your bed. Close your eyes, like I have closed mine.
And not think.

Do not think about the beggars who chased you at the market today.
Do not think about the poor living on the roadside
Do not think about how your brother failed his exams
Do not think about the morning's feud between your parents
Do not think about your teacher who told you to write that article again
Do not think about your future job
Do not think about the monuments in your city
Do not think about that camera you cannot buy
Do not think about the broken relationships
Do not think about those empty promises

Do not think about that wrapper you threw on the street
Do not think about that mosquito you accidentally swallowed
Do not think about how hollow your soul is
Do not think about narrating your eulogy before anybody else could
Do not think about people who do not exist anymore
Do not think about the forgotten ATM pin.

The Promenade

Forget everything. Everything. Yes, Everything.

Oh, don't remember me too.
Just close your eyes.

Concentrate on those whirls & circles.
They'll hypnotize you.
They'll force you to push all your thoughts away.
Thinking makes a man wise.
Not thinking makes a man free.

Every Other Day

//Same old. Same old.//

Everything in this world is so trite.
The mangoes ripe.
Our jibber-jabber never ends.
Every day we lie to people, tell them that we love them.
We drink water because we would die otherwise.
And stub the cigarette butts on walls,
blackening their souls.
Telling each other we want to spend our lives together over
coffee;
we are on a date after all.

Fighting early morning because veggies didn't cook right.
Or because last night we found out about each other's infidelity.
The bosses kicked our asses.

And the condoms, well chuck it.
Our sacred vows are already taking a backseat.
You told me about Nietzsche and Einstein and Bergman and
Vinci.
I told you about Romeo and Juliet and the Seventh Seal.
We are in a loop.
Doing everything all over again.
My third or no, fourth relationship, I am still the same.
Your eighth, or maybe second or even first
Still,

the same old, the same old, the same old.
We never change.
We remain the same.
Is change the only constant?
What a joke!
We are so fucking hacky.

//Refuge//

I am at a party, I never wanted to go to.
A glass of Chardonnay keeping me company.
A long lost friend spots me,
And asks me what's up?
I smile awkwardly.
My face flushes red.
Painting my time with bloody red.
Confused, my yellow, thrawn teeth greet her.
My dry lips open pleasantly.
I hug her with half heartedly.
Oblivious to my discomfort,
She blabbers about the good old days.
"8 years!" she exclaimed.
"8 years," I said.
I dread small talks, interrogations, and exaggerations.
That's what people offer.
That's what she wasted my time on.
Then,
Uneasy silence and half a glass Chardonnay.

"I need to go to the loo... Will be back in a while."
[Oh, never. Never]
I leave my glass of leftover Chardonnay,
I cut our friendship in two halves,

One half fills my heart with relief,
One half directs her to someone else.
I rush towards the loo,
I shut myself in this parallel world.
Light my cigarette with my fire,
And smoke to pacify my violent, stormy nerves.
What a wreck!
My skin still feels itchy,
Why did I come crawling to this party?
The inevitable journey from Obligations to Neurosis to Malfunctions.
It's impossible for me to bear-human interactions anymore.
I go to work and hide in the loo.
I come here and do it again.
Thank God these safe havens exist.
I would rather spend my time here,
on this uncomfortable commode,
Rather go out and blabber incessantly.
This is my escape from this world full of shit.
Shitty people blithering about shitty things.
God, they perplex me.
God, how do I elope this place without being questioned?
I hope nobody knocks this door, To puke on my only retreat.
These creamy, coarse walls know my secret.
Might even judge me for being foolish.
Indiscreet.
But do I care?
No.

//Choice//

She was gifted.
She had the virtue to control everybody's mind.
Fix everything.
Save Lives.

But when prejudice touched her path;
He invaded her conscience.
Her blessing changed its shape into a bane.
And She?

Paralyzed for Life.

//You need to remember some things in life//

There are times you lose confidence in you,
you stop respecting yourself,
you think other people make you happy,
that your perfect relationship or perfect job is everything
you need to fuel your longings,
It's not.
If you are perpetually sad and trying to elope what is right in
front you then it's not because of the others.
It is you.
You are the cynosure of everything in your life and
that's exactly why you need to gather yourself together,
heal yourself and love yourself.
As simple as it sounds, as intricate everything beyond is.
You need to love your heartbreaks, your failures, your
losses, your scars.

You are not perfect, but you crave for perfection;
Loving yourself doesn't mean writing yourself long letters
or continually staring in the mirror like a maniac
(I mean it's not that bad okay?)
You need to feel yourself,
Things cannot work your way and you have to admit that,
Just don't lose yourself in the quest for success.
You already are a success.

Stop whining

I am not asking you to settle with what you have,

Work hard for things you want and don't work hard if you

do not want anything.

Your choice.

Completely.

But don't be hard on yourself because it's not the others you

spend your nights crying for, it's you.

You wail endlessly for your own self.

You blame yourself for things you didn't do because you

want to be goody-two-shoes.

To hell with that.

Period.

Oh! Now, don't you deny it?

Don't be afraid to accept the truth as it is because, in the end,

all that matters is how honest you were with yourself.

And you have to be honest with the people you love.

If you truly want to love yourself, be honest at least.

It's hard I know, but that's what loving yourself is about and

that's what being content is about.

You can never even see the light of happiness entering your

threshold if you keep your doors locked.

It's okay if you are sad, but there has to be a reason, and if

that's not the case you really have some self-love problems.

Trusting yourself wins half of the battle for you.

Really.
Trust me.
I would never lie to you.
Why would I?

//She couldn't rhyme//

She couldn't rhyme,
The art of music was missing,
Her soul lacked that rhythm.
She manipulates words,
Manipulated her poems,
Worth contemplating once.

Possibility is,
One would not understand its depth.
The emotions attached to it.
It's true those words are plainly arranged.
A certain melody,
Embellishes the poetry.
She lacked it.

Hers were merely short fables.
Stories of Love.
Stories of Hatred.
Stories of Fragrance.
Stories of fatality.
love hatred fragrance.
And, maybe beyond.

Not musical.
Yet meaningful.

//Trust//

There was a time
Somewhere in the past
Where people simply deceived
Each other
Mocked love
Cheated life
Weren't loyal enough
Generations passed by
Time revolutionized in full swing
Faith, in the ineffable world
Was never paramount

An Eternity remained thirsty for trust.

//Dahlias//

There was this girl,
Beautiful and Naïve,
Who loved Dahlias.

She bought them daily,
Her room was crammed with countless of them.
Her mother asked her "who gives you these every day?"
No one does.
No one ever did.
Why did she buy those dahlias?
Every single day?

She would click those beautiful flowers,
It was part of her routine.

#flowers
1 heart, 2 heart,
People don't care about flowers!
Followers began to decline.
Virtual and Real.
Her friends unfollowed her.
Virtual and Real.

"Why do you put up these flowers?"
They all ask her why she loved Dahlias?
Why only dahlias?

She told them she loved dahlias for their profoundness.
She loved their color.
She loved their fragrance.
A fragrance of nothingness.

She loved the way they looked at her.
She loved the way they whispered kind things into her ears.
She was grateful to them for their generosity.
For saving her when nothing else could.

She manifested her love for dahlias in front of everyone
and no one ever understood why!
Why do you have to tell the world?

If you love a flower keep to yourself.
Nobody really wants to know.
Are you in love with someone?
Who's giving you these dahlias?
Why do you click pictures of flowers you bought on your
own and upload it on social media?
Is there any story behind?
There must be something!
There has to be something!
Come on tell us now!
Don't be shy!

No!
No!
No!
No, there's no romance behind it.
No guy is giving it to me.
I buy them myself.
Am I not entitled to do that?
To bring me these beautiful flowers?

My dahlias love me for who I am.
And, so do I.
They don't pour unnecessary questions on me.
They don't judge me.
They don't ask me anything.
They listen to me during the times of despair.
When I want to kill myself I look at those dahlias and smile.
They give me the strength to live.
To survive.
They don't call me names,
Think I'm a slut.
They don't scold me when I mess up.
I am not a laughing stock for them.
They understand that I am different.
They know I am unique.
They help me heal.
I wish humans could do that.
I wish we could heal each other.
Aren't we all just too damaged?

Aren't we?
Non-sense!
Non-sense!
Non-sense!

You don't know my story, bitch.
You can't heal me.
You cannot know what I go through.
You don't know how ashamed I am of my scars.
I need to punch someone!
I need to pull someone's hair!
I need to shout! I need to tell this world I am above them!

I need to talk.
I just need to talk to someone.
But I guess 'someone' doesn't exist.

We have our own Dahlias in life.
Don't we?
Poetry, pen, the purr of a cat,
Endless, Endless Dahlias
All over the place.
Endless, Endless Dahlias
All over my heart.

I wish my people were like Dahlias too.
I wish my people watched me slit my wrist instead of these
kind Dahlias.

I wish dahlias could speak, for they know my true pain, my agony.
I wish dahlias could do something I couldn't.
I keep wishing on my death chair. I just keep wishing.
Oh, my Dahlias! How lovely art thou?
How kind art thou?
For you know my blood had your scent.
Everywhere.
Everywhere.
Everywhere.
Such an ecstatic death.
Dahlias smiled.

//Enervated//

Every time I sit to write,
To create,
I feel the lack of originality creeping up my spine,
Silently.

Thoughts are a collage of ambiguity,
Poetry becomes a wordless journey,
And prose, as forgettable as people lost in wars.
There's bloodshed in my mind.
Tears stream continually,
Can't resort to sleep,
Enervated, exhausted, drained.
Introspection on a piece of paper failed.
The honor of writers and writings,
Are lost in the emotionless clogged pool.
You know, in the end, we take some of our valuables in the
grave,
My thoughts and I will be buried in the same way.
And I wish they do.
If even a single thought survived,
This universe will burn down,
Sag with shame.

//The Tryst with Antonyms//

Those star-crossed eyes were searching for bliss.
They continuously stared at the lamp on the other side of the
street in hope.
But soon those wandering eyes were forced to embrace the
dusky darkness.
The eyes believe that darkness consist a tinge of light.
The light of hope.
The light of love.
Darkness is utterly spellbinding because it brings relief to
the wrecked soul.
All the great men and artists would have never achieved
anything without darkness.
The lamp is a pretentious source of light.
It is solitary as it appears but that's where this world is
delusional.
The lamp, the guide during the dark times has a deeper
friendship with the mighty night.
If there weren't night, a lamp's soul would have been extinct.
Nobody reckons the value of light without darkness.
Obscurity is entwined in the world.
So is the concept of Light and Darkness
The antonyms are inevitable.
Always.

//Liberation, Glory, Buoyancy, and Transformation//

My existence is referred to as an unnatural crime in the
books of law.
My preference is referred to as insanity around the country.
My existence is referred to as a torment by my beloved
parents.
My company is referred to as disgrace by this society.
My talent is referred to as a waste by whosoever
encompasses my reality.
My identity is referred to as a joke funnier than the clowns.
My style is referred to as an impact of my 'foes'.
My success is referred to as a thorn in everyone's route.
My happiness is referred to as a curse for millions.
My faith is referred to as a mockery of the Almighty.
My mind is referred to as a sordid place acknowledged by
numerous doctors.
My soul is referred to as a dark black void for the sake of
religion.
My love is referred to as bizarre, whenever I confess.
My life is referred to as a nuisance every time I breathe.
The sour affliction I am,
Makes me unacceptable by all and one.
What I have been 'referred to as',
Murders me slowly.

Steadily.
Bit by bit.
Everyday.
The path I chose,
has been declared sinful & inhuman in the name of God.
But you are forgetting that you don't know 'it' yet.
No matter how much you despise my rights.
There's one paradigm I will always affirm:
"Discriminating me, won't make your miserable lives any better."
All we need is to open ourselves.

//Fascination//

Near the embankment of a river,
I saw the swan princess,
Her beauty spellbound me.
I walked close to her.
As I reached closer & closer,
Her figure became more prominent.
She was mindlessly fondling her hands over green, fresh grass.
As I was about to touch her,
She disappeared,
And I realized,
She was a mirage.
And I wondered,
Why all the beauty on this earth
Is surreal?

//Art.//

She was Aztec in nature.
He was a portrait.
She belonged to the mellow tribes.
He was all about profound cities.
They were completely disparate from each other.
Yet, one thing connected them
Art.

//Agonized Wolf//

This agony of being incapable,
Caged in shackles,
A mad, mad wolf.
I howl, I wail,
I wait for the full moon night.
I am lunatic, I am artless,
I shout to break-away from my own head.
I feel broken, I feel shattered
A piece of disappointment
I wish my unrequited prayers,
To levitate in the infinity,
Be answered with a boon,
To be free.

//Seclusion//

I cloistered myself behind the walls of illusion
Confined me in my own imaginary world
Magic secluded me from reality
And I escaped the bitterness of truth
Relieved from my nemesis.
I was relieved from life.

//What happens here stays here//

"How are you," he said.

"I am fine, thank you," she said.

"It doesn't seem so," he said.

"No, nothing. Why do you think so?" she said.

"You don't seem fine," he said.

"Well, I don't think so. I'm all right," she said.

"I think you're covering up," he said.

"What? There's nothing wrong, stop poking!" She said.

"I can see it on your face, you're not okay," he said.

"Well, let me tell you, mister, it's none of your business,"
she said.

"I know it isn't, but still I'm concerned," he said.

A drop of tear fell from her eyes,

Washing her cheeks.

Her kohl smudged,

Accentuating the baggy circles under her eyes.

He found his answers.

"I just want to go out and get hit by a truck. And never
wake up again," she said.

"Why? What's wrong? I don't understand" He said.

"I want you to see how I turn into fragments of dust," she said.

He was baffled.

She was vengeful.

"I cannot see you like this," he said.

"You brought me here," she said.

"I would never want you to do that to yourself," he said.
"What you want, doesn't matter anymore," she said.
"Baby, things cannot happen the way you want," he said.
"They never happened the way I wanted to be," she said.
She got up.
Rose above.
Called a numen.
The winds blew.
The tides came.
And she turned into ashes.
He saw all this.
And closed his eyes.

To open them again.
In a different, estranged place.
He knew nothing of.
She was there, amidst the crowd of thousands.

He couldn't believe his eyes.
He couldn't believe her eyes.

//Dead-end//

His silhouette drew a peculiar shadow on the ground.
She kept following his silhouette,
The shadow led her to a mysterious route,
They kept on walking.
One behind the other.
Soon she reached the edge,
Raging, colossal tides of the sea staring at them,
That somber spirit melded with the dead end.

Now it was her turn.

A story before we begin...

A firefly entered a pitch dark house.
A house, untouched for many years. A house full of beautiful antiques and pictures. A house of memories.

"This would have been such a beautiful house earlier," she said to herself. She was the only source of light in that ruined place. It was completely destroyed as if somebody has cursed the place.

She could feel someone approaching her. Walking towards her. Every step was confident and firm. He was the owner of the house. Tall and sightly, crafted with profound intricacy.

She was in awe of this man. He stood in front of her, admiring her light. She thought to leave, after all, she was an intruder. While flying her way back, the owner of the house stopped her and asked her to stay. He wanted her to stay back. The only source of light in this dark, solitary house.

She was elated!
Her flight was joyous. She stayed back. Her gratitude towards him knew no bounds. She was thankful, he let her stay. They had an instant deep-rooted connection, a strange

attachment like their souls have known each other all along. As if, they were meant to be together. To share one roof for an entire lifetime.

Her light illuminated their lives. The house echoed with their laughter. The walls were painted with the color of affection. Every day, they danced merrily.
That house wasn't the same anymore.
Love wasn't the same anymore.

Bliss In Love

//Oh, Love!//

My heart raced expeditiously.
Pounced a zillion times.
He approached closer & closer,
His hands stroked my hair,
His nose found the right place to stay,
His lips conquering my eyes.
I could feel him breathing over me.
I caressed his cheeks with my fingertips,
Brushed his hair further.
Touched his shoulders,
Slowly, he gazed at me.
I glanced back.
Frozen in the embrace,
Our ears heard the serenade of love.
Solely played for us.

//Wave//

The boy I love,
has cigarette burns.
His father had a bad
temper, when he was
young. His father took
it all out on him and
his poor mother.
Now, that he
has cancer,
he has mellowed
down. The boy I love,
still takes care of him.
Looks after his father's
medical expense, toils
hard to provide for
his family and
never
complains.
Every time,
after making love,
I touch his scars, and
see the wounds that
have healed over time,
but left their imprint
on his memory.

The boy I love,
never looks at
anybody
with spite.
He is innocent,
charming and
everything nice
you can think of,
on the exterior. Inside,
he is still struggling with
his demons, hushing them,
whispering in their ears
that forgiveness is the
greatest, if not most
satisfying thing to do.
That he does not
need to strangle
his father to
death.
That living
like a
parasite
is his biggest
punishment.
The boy I love,
knew revenge.

//A Forever//

It was a very precise encounter with him.
I just passed by his side.
Glanced at him for a moment.
Seconds later, he was lost in the drizzle of the rain.
His fragrance created an obscure image of him in my mind.
That brief encounter was enough to make my heart race.
His identity, unknown to me,
His vague image was enough to be loved for an entire lifetime.
This little tale seems absolutely foolish.

But, just wonder, how lovely it is to fall for a complete stranger.
To be in love and remain estranged forever.
All complexities diminish.
The fright of separation never bothers you.
Perhaps, love never loses its sheen.
I think I have found my 'eternity.'

//Magic of Love//

I am in love with you,
with your flaws,
with your agony,
your bruises, those deep cuts.
I am in love with you,
the way you murmur in your sleep,
the way you enjoy your coffee.
Your honesty, thy joy.
I am in love with you,
the way you shed your tears in my arms,
the way you hold me.
Your energy, that vivacity.
I am in love with you,
as many as times I can repeat these words,
if there's ever anything deeper than the ocean, it's us.
Together, we enchant the world with miracles.
The magic of love.

//Hypnosis//

There's a strong magnetic pull I feel,
Attracting me towards a light.

Your eyes being my cynosure,
Pulling me, towards you.

You have the strings,
To control my world.

You are my gravity,
I need you to hold this earth.

You have cured my heart,
Healed all my scars.

Embraced me softly,
Unfastening all my inhibitions and doubts.

I let you devour my being,
Let me bleed underwater.

I want to merge with your soul,
Become a part of you,
Be in your blood.

Drink me, oh beloved!
Drown in my beauty.

This is what you've done to me,
Hypnotized me with your love.

//Prodigy//

As we move forward,
Osculate,
Our fragrances fall for each other,
Our unison is fiery,
We breathe densely,
Our arms tightly packed,
Eyes locked with each other,

Still.

Words left a lacuna in our book.
Sentences left incomplete,
The darkness wasn't shallow,
The air felt meaningful,
Betwixt we realized,
We were just meant to be,
Together,
Beyond all superficial surfaces,
Love is a prodigy indeed.

//Reunion//

They met.
Met after a long, long time.
Years flew by since they saw each other.
It was like a gap of a lifetime has been refilled,
They stood still,
Even the wind couldn't move them,
Sparkling were their eyes,
Nervous were their hands,
The whole galaxy watched them shining away,
Guilt,
Remorse,
Hesitation,
Nervousness,
All these words lost their souls when they met,
They met.

To stay together for another lifetime.

//The Saviour//

There will be a lot of hurdles
Abundant ordeals,
Myriad of thorns,
Uneven roads,
Infinite difficulties,
A consistent, peculiar terror.

But I,
Will protect love.

From the clutches of Fear,
I will relieve love.

For I refuse to give up.

Love will be victorious.

Hail Love!
Together, we'll save Love!

//Nectar of Ecstasy//

I saw him holding me.
We both wearing white.
Immaculate clothes.
La Vie En Rose in the background.
A breezy dance.

We both lost in each other's arms.
Swaying gently with every beat.
With every melody.

With every rhythm.
Carefree.
Boundless.

We performed on the stage of life.
The stars meeked away,
Evacuating the sky.
The moon, a gleeful spectator.
And we,
Made for each other.

//From Heaven, To Love//

Our strange odyssey started.
We walked through the ridges and rocks.
Elevated mountains carried us,
We briskly eloped aisle of heaven.
The slope,
transcending into the ocean of sorrow.
Thalassic caverns, our home, will scarcely be warm.

But there's a distinct faith residing within us.
Together we can illuminate the gloomiest night.
Radiance of our love will brighten every darkness.
Love can strife all ordeals.

//Miracle of Trust//

One night,
We must lay down by each other's side.
Naked.
Facing each other.
Neither to make love,
Nor to sleep.
Just to stay awake.
Quiet.
The dusky room should feel
our silence.
The only sound should be of the
enchanting air.

We look at each other,
Endlessly.
Intensely.
Eye to eye.
Heart to heart.
Stare for long hours.
Do nothing.

Nothing at all.
Appreciate this time.
Stay static.
Clench each other with our eyes.

After sometime,
I know,
Our faces will be embellished with smiles.
That smile,
Will be the most genuine expression ever endowed.
The room,
The air,
The bed,
Will witness a miracle.
The miracle of trust.

Love.
It knows what magic is.

//Violinist//

Never did I imagine
That I would wait
To listen you play the violin
By the golden gate.

Your melancholy was apparent
With the symphony, you played
As if you were once youthful and gallant
Before you hide behind your music's shade.

Like a tree, your music relaxes you
You never see it as a chore
Its poignancy makes people blue
Nobody ever asks for more

But I love what you create
For there's hope at least music will not leave you desolate.

//To Feel Eternally//

That dawn changed their lives forever...

The moon shone lustrously.
The stars glistened splintering the dark night.
That night was indeed shimmering.

He just sat beside her,
Wondering why the night appeared to be so beautiful.
He silently looked at her to ask the same,
There was a peculiar sparkle in her eyes as the answer to his question.
He was in the awe of that twinkle of her eyes.
Maybe it was not about the moons and stars at all.

//A forgettable couplet//

Even if you never tell me
what is bothering your mind.
I'll know the storm that
Keeps you awake all night.

//Devour me with Love//

That's how writers blow life into the dead.
They observe the most negligible atom.
They sew particles of dust into magic.
They glorify even a thread of your hair.
They beautify destruction.
They mystify miracles.
They touch souls.

That's what you did to me.
Tore me apart.
Broke me into infinite fragments.
Devoured me.
Conjoined my dreams with yours.
Constructed my reality.
Made me yours.
Loved me.

//Hope//

You prove me wrong every night,
And I, shamelessly, still wake up
With hope in my eyes every morning.
Hope to reconcile with you.
Hope to ignite your heart with love.
Hope, that one day, we will see the sun together.
Hope, that one night, moon blushes at seeing us together.
Hope.

//Midnight Thoughts//

My poetry, prose, little fables, ability to think,
Vanished into the dark woods.
My surreal world collapsed.
With you gone, the light of my life diminished.
And the earth flooded with incoherent, hostile thoughts.
My words stopped breathing.
My afreets became stronger.
Quenched their thirst with my blood.
If you ever remember me.
Visit my grave for my thoughts lie there.
In the dark wooden coffin, my soul is cloistered.
Ashes of my dreams buried beneath the soil.
That one poem dearest to me is engraved on the headstone.
Bend a little towards me and drop some ink.
My laughter will echo in your ears.
My smile will flash in front of your eyes.
My fragile hands will hold you.
Perhaps, my love, you will feel my anguish.
You will narrate my story to all.
How I tried to succumb to the devil.
How he entered my mouth slowly.
How he whipped my skin.
Gave me sour wounds, made me bleed.
How he controlled my bones.
How he aggressively abused my soul every day.

Gulped me down his throat.
I know tears would trickle down from your eyes,
when you'll hear of my destruction.
I will wipe your tears, give you a peck.
Darling, I will love from distance.

//Discovery//

Scraped the debris of heart
Lifted the ruins
Took me to a place
Not a single living soul knew.

In every grain of memories
A name is engraved
With each cadence
It pounds with a deafening sound.

A speck of hope aroused
Exhumed from the soil of dead
Little did we know, these vibrations
will become synonymous with life.

These reverberations, these tenors
Rhythm of totality
When we danced,
danced with the prophets.

Imagine.
This world.
With me.
See what I see.
And you will know.

Growing bitter...

In the season of spring, a perky butterfly flew amidst the exotic flowers. There she met a thorn. The thorn wounded her dreadfully, pierced her violet wings. She was hurt. All the attempts to get up, pull everything together and fly, were futile. She couldn't endure the pain. Her world crashed down in seconds.

She was agonized by the fact that she had to live without her majestic wings. She thought, her fate was unkind.

Her loved ones abandoned her after a while. Nobody chose to look after her and help her recover, they had their own lives after all. They all flew away. The injury took her everything away. One accident and her life changed into a bane. Nothing provided her solace. The reality of being left over in a desert of solitude was unbearable.

Seasons changed. Some days, the sun shone brightly. Some days, it rained heavily. Some days the colors faded. Some days, the colors rejuvenated. She watched everything changes from a distance. She couldn't participate in the magnificence of nature. Helpless as a rock, a mere spectator. Her beautiful heaven had collapsed like dominoes.

No music could heal her. She stopped enjoying her surroundings like she used to. She stopped feeling gleeful.

The gloominess was initially bitter but, soon she accepted and later, assimilated it within her. She elicited sorrow to dwell in her mind.

"Life is a sleazy murderer," she thought.

The Salty Ocean

//Inevitable Twins//

That night,

Her sobs were audible.

I was terrified.

She was pouring her heart, from her eyes.

And, I was paralyzed.

She was dark and depressed.

I was naive and afraid.

We both resided in the same body.

But nothing could help us meet.

Tragedy.

//Destined//

They were searching for a
a peaceful place to hide.
Hide to make love.
Make love to know
where the thorns bloom.
Thorns, that strengthens a relationship
A relationship to live together.
'Live Together'

That's what they were not destined to.

//Corpse//

Pale Skin.
Blank Eyes.
Parched Lips.
Numb Hands.
She is a very active corpse.

//A Nightmare//

The starvation in the Ogre's eyes terrified her.
She was afraid of that giant monster.
She ran to save her & reached the end of the woods.
It was 7 AM.
Nightmare Over!

But running away from demons never ended.

//An ode to someone I loved//

i
This is an ode.
An ode to something I loved.
Someone, actually.

ii
No, he isn't a random boy I met at school,
Neither isn't he that random boy's friend,
Who became my rebound,
Eventually I fell for him as well,
Nor it is about the boy I truly loved once,
The one who entered the territory of this heart,
With grenades hanging around his spine,
like summer fruits.

iii
This is about a man.
You see, relationships you pick hardly mean anything.

iv
This about him, who wiped my tears when I whimpered,
when my dolls broke.
But never wiped my tears when I whimpered, when my
heart broke.

This is about him, who fought with anyone, who even eyed
my cocoon.
Who eloped my side, when I entered this battle with the
world.
This is about him, my mustached hero, the one who
brawled with ghosts, vampires and poisonous snakes.
The one who dragged my paralyzed mother out of the
house by her hair.

v

This is about him,
Who told me I could be anything I wanted.
The one who poisoned my life with infinite judgments and
unreasonable expectations.
This is about him,
Who was selflessly in love with me.
The one who now counts his contributions to my
upbringing, sometimes, calls it a loan.
This is about him,
Who knew when I breathed, knew my heartbeats.
The one who doesn't know me anymore.

vi

I don't think I really need to tell you who he is.
I think you know who he is.

All of this just makes me wonder how people change.
Or is it all an act?
I can never tell.

//Walls//

They crumbled.
They crumbled every night.
Together but separately.
To feel each other's presence,
Was a distant dream.
But pain scribbled unison on invisible walls.
Invisible walls of fate.

//Debris//

She was a destroyed piece of Art.
And, he was her creator.
He crafted her & forgot.
A wooden shelf kept her alive.

And she, now lying under rubble.
Wishes that he recalls her someday to
Save her from the ruins.
But fate,
Her heart died a death,
nobody would remember.

//A forgotten bird//

She was caged,
She collapsed every day,
She was chastised every night.
Nobody quench her thirst,
Nobody fed her,
Nobody helped her,
Not even the one who caged her.

Cruelty.

//An incomplete fable//

i

Here's a story of an old man,
An artist who bled ink.
He stayed in his beaten, blue caravan,
And wrote tales that could make a heart sink.

ii

There was this one fable,
He was never able to finish,
About the dead cat under the table,
Poisoned with the goldfish.

iii

The story was beyond absurd,
Call it his madness.
He dreamt of a mellifluous mockingbird,
Leading him into sadness.

iv

His poor lover waited for him,
Singing a winter interlude.
His eyes had turned grey and grim,
He saw the arrival of an inevitable feud.

V

Alas, his lover gave up.

He was tired of bearing his grief.

He gave him the death cup.

For him to die silently, with some relief.

//Pain//

Your eyes that once saw,
The dream of never letting me go of your arms.
Those arms, once held me tight,
Have turned so cold.

Intimacy collapsed.

Continuing to erode,
Every other day,
Every single moment.

In every breath I take,
I see you farther than before.

//Solace//

My soul has been writhing in agony.
Those strong echo of from the past, haunt me.
My wilting soul needs solace.
But, nobody provides me with this relief.
Not even God.

Banished from the heaven.
Vanquished by Hell.

Catastrophe.
Catastrophe.
Catastrophe.

//A lesson to remember//

He was a pretentious man
Held a rhetoric paradigm towards life.

Flaunted his journey around
The world with flair and flamboyance.

Everybody listened carefully to his tales.
Came from places to listen him share his capsule of fiction.

But nobody turned up on the day of his funeral,
Even though he lived an enigmatic life,
Nobody was present to intonate his eulogy.

Friends, you & your stories always die alone.

//Nowhere to go//

I once wanted to take refuge,
In your thoughts.
Unfortunately,
I realised your mind is a wretched place as soon as I
stepped in.

The idea suffocates me now
Look where my innocence landed me…

It feels as if I am dwelling
In monstrous woods that spell doom every time I blink.

These woods have imprisoned me.
I am trapped, beyond salvage.

What do I even do?
There's nowhere else to go.

//Hourglass//

I lost my art.
The art to express me.
The wise words from the sun.

My poetry has turned into a valley,
A valley of lost words.

As if sand flows in an hourglass,
Yet, the grains will never be the same.

The moon will never be the metaphor for love,
Just its ordinary self.

And sorrow is the new vogue,
It keeps my eyelids closed with pain,
My heart awake in agony and dismay.

With wars in my head,
If words ever washed out in the rain.
I could never be the same again.

//She was the only one.//

She was the only one,
He ever loved.
She was the only one,
He ever admired.
She was the only one,
He looked up to during troubled times.
She was the only one,
He wished to be present by his side.
She was the only one.

And I was a mute spectator.
Who loved him hysterically.

But that love,
Was a stark burning black hole in my soul.

//Mansions//

His eyes were grave and deep.
His nose slender and sleek.
His lips were firm.
My hands wanted to explore all his demeanors.
His flawless cheeks.
His dense and curly hair.
His magnificent heart.
I kissed him all over.
I loved him all over.

I roused from my slumber wide awake.
Nostalgia has a tomstone to its name.
All my dreams for him,
Were mere mansions in maudlin air.

//To Let Her Go//

I could hear her sobbing endlessly over the phone.
She wanted me to leave and never return.
Not even in her memories.
It was making her weak.
Turning her into a leach.

I imagined her to be on her knees,
Craving for peace.
She asked me to let her go.
Let her go, forever.

I knew I was the reason.
All that pain I gave her.
The heartache she wasn't entitled to.

I wasn't powerful enough to mend the circumstances.

I had to let her go.

She kept dying every second,
Wailing,
Hovering.

I felt something surging from my eyes.
I couldn't wrap her in my arms.
Even if I wanted to.
I had killed her faith after all.
I had killed the love in her.

//Trapped//

"Stop taking over my mind,"
"You cannot turn me into a bigot"!

Devil smiled.

"I wish it was me,
disorienting you from the goodness,
Alas, it's you," he said.

She was taken aback.
Bewildered.

Nothing to cleanse her soul.
The departure of knowledge, palpable.

//Always//

Your memories always agonize me.
Every time you cross my mind,
I adore your smooth symphony.
Every time your shadow overcasts my stirring corpse,
My inclination towards you,
makes me let go of my inhibitions.
Our paths were separated years ago,
you still wake me up with your far aglow,
How you deserted me,
That road we walked on together,
When our forever wasn't a lie.
It felt the journey would lead us home,
But it left this unusual pain behind.
To me, you're a ghostly figure now.

Somewhere, 'always' lost its candour.

//Deprived of empathy//

She was forsaken,
In a house full of people,
Relinquished by all.

She spent her life all by herself, alone.
Surrounded by people who were to wooden to care.
Nothing could save her from desolation.

Her spirit was cut loose.
She surrendered her joy.
She accepted the slaughter, behold.

Secluded from Love.
Secluded from Life.
Tragedy won over her plight.

Relinquished,
She left dejected.
She, now understood.
Life is not always kind.

//Fate//

The urge to see you just once,
Still trespasses my mind every day.

I weave dreams with my eyes wide open,
Set locations for the perfect date,

Smile at my own reveries.

Alas, my fate!

My longing ends every night,
With a sour pinch of disappointment,
Each night, teardrops religiously water my cheeks with
sorrow.

And I know,
I will never be able to see you again.

///The eternal hope//

She waited for him,
Waited for her beloved,
To arrive at her threshold,
Call out her name.

She dreamed of running into his arms.

But he,
He never arrived.

She waited all day long.
Waited for someone who didn't exist.

Hope.

It gave her a reason to survive,
To wait.

Perhaps, this viciousness will never end for her.
She will step into the grave, with hope in her soul.
This wait is persistent

Even, after her she gave up on her life.

//The story of my tears//

My tears are cloistered,
Caged inside my eyes.
They want to break free,
Burst out with one pinch.
But their fate is as bad as mine.

We are barred from following,
Our own will.

//Winner of ruins//

I stand alone, a victorious gladiator in the field.
Challenging the dead to rise from other world.
Whispering the sonnets for deceased in the reaper's ears.
The battle was horrendous,
I remember their fingers bleeding,
Throats slit explicitly in war,
The swords blinded my vision.

The blood-thirsty arms waited to slay each other,
To separate all the children of God from their beloved,
The sight tormented me intrinsically,
Life is a woe.

I died long before I was declared dead,
I plead to grant me one day to live,
I don't wish to sleep this early,
But, my eyes hurt to lay awake.

//Dread the night//

Late at night,
I introspect the time bygone,
Beneath the blanket,
Curled up to clench my thoughts together.
My past unravels with galactic shimmers,

I witness it all.

I daydream of a future,
Wondering of all the remorse I shall face again.
I analyze my present hopelessly,
To find a tinge of joy in the days I'm living.

My eyes create their own conclusion,
With tides of tears.

My lips pray silently,
Wishing for my beloved to sleep by my side.
My feet tremble,
Hands quiver,
The mind struggles,
To decode life.

And heart?
The heart is doing, what it does the best.
Blaming itself for what I go through,
Every night.

//Love, deceives//

Love, the only thing I asked for.
The only feeling I'm deprived of.

There's betrayal everywhere,
Fire on all the streets.

Ashes of people scattered everywhere,
Crushed beneath every step I take.

I have given up on love.
It's just another peculiar word to me now.

I have tried my heart at it.

One day, the idea itself will suffocate me to death.
I beg to drown. I can't bear it anymore.

Paint my own destruction,
With my own hands.

The beauty of love deceives.
Like every other beautiful thing.

//The Eulogy//

I never had a chance
To describe me the way
I always wanted to.
Everyone had a piece of mine.
A lie I told to myself and others.
Not even a tinge of honesty,
Not even a reflection of my soul.
Being victorious, the sole objective.
Being wise, never crossed the conscience.
But, on my last day;
The most awaited,
The most certain day.
The day I had to stop masquerading.
The day I had to openly vent out my melancholy.
The day I am truthful about my own existence.

The wind of autumn awaited for me to shed my leaves.
To display my original hues,
Be it shallow,
Be it bright,
I had a chance to depict all my plight.
I was on the edge,
That point ahead of despotism and hatred.

Where being kind weighed the most.
I,
Manifest my own eulogy.

//Tale of Lost Fortune//

She, the denizen of an imaginary world
Ran and Ran and Ran,
From the Ultimate Truth.
The ethereal world,
Was calling out her name.
Profusely.
Continuously.
Chasing her.

Back & Forth.
Back & Forth.

She was out of her breath,
Stopped for a moment to rest.
Lethargy took its toll.
The reality was quick,
Captured her in a jiffy.

Chained her.
Kept her close.
Really close.
She wailed.
She sobbed.
She begged
Her efforts, all in vain.

Reality beamed in victory.
After all, it captured her successfully.
She had to surrender to the veracious fate.
This made her lose the loveliest thing of all.
A thing of ecstasy indeed.
The only thing she never wanted to mislay.
Magic.

//Fate triumphs//

Everybody stood still around her,
Disarmed.
Wailing.
Helpless.
She was brawling alone.
Unaided.
With an unrecognized power.
A power pulling her away from the people she loved,
People surrounding her at that very moment.
She fought.
Struggled for her life.
Battled really hard.
But in the end, she lost.
They lost.
Everybody lost.
Except the Omnipresent.
She turned into a pale blue corpse.
Her spirit was snatched successfully.
Mortals are repeatedly forfeited by certainty.
Death pervasively arrives on its own time.
Destiny is always victorious.

//Sacred Imaginations//

By the end of the day,
I lie down and take your name.

You appear in front of me,
In my sacred imagination.

You hold me close,
And whisper,
It's all good,
Fall asleep darling,
I am here.

But,
I always wake up alone.

The truth is you're not here,
Or there, or anywhere.

It's just me
Who is here, or there or everywhere.

//I have something to say//

I thank God,
For the destiny, he engraved in my palms.

But now,
I wish to free myself from his disposal.

Leave for a long solitary journey.

When you receive what you search for...

While searching for her soul, she became a poet.

She wrote extensively, wholeheartedly. The paper witnessed the catharsis of her heart. She weaved beautiful sonnets and stories of love. Calling out the name of God, her papers brimmed with miracles.

One day, a pensive, kind phantom came into her dream. He was wearing a white robe and a turban. He knocked her room's door. She opened it and was puzzled. She thought to herself, "who was he?"

He was radiant, glowing like a river. His aura had the tranquillity of the mountains. Beguiled by his appearance, she asked him about his identity.
He smiled. She smiled.
They both knew. Her prayers were answered.
God himself came to acknowledge her.
He blessed her with the gift of enlightenment. She accepted the gift with respect and responsibility. But acceptance of the gift doesn't help you in knowing the supreme truth. Such gifts are not meant to be decorated in the cupboards.
They need to be experienced and shared.

Mysticism makes you a whale.

Calm and Determined.

You swim across the endless ocean of knowledge.

Magic makes you a bird.

Sharp and Intellectual. You soar high into the infinite sky to know who you are, and what you are made of.

Miracles happen.

When that spirit you have always known, meets you, you accept each other, make love and finally rest together.

This is what eternity truly means.

The Magic Unravels

//Feeling depressed? Good.//

Did you ever feel
Your hands going numb,
Your feet paralyzed,
Your eyes losing vision,
Your mouth drying,
Your loss of words,
Your skin turning pale,
Your nerves freezing,
Your mind flabbergasted,
Your heart clueless,
Your body failing,

Any of it? Ever?

You're lucky if you did.

Despair is an undiscovered art.
Poetry lies in solitude.
Strength is discovered in chaos.
Love is nourished inside the famished.
Sorrow unveils magic.

//Poetry//

It's not just a collection of words,
Set in logical, chronological order.
They are emotions.
Floating in one's soul.
The abreaction of heart,
Waiting to be said aloud.

Believers wait for all their lives,
To unravel an undiscovered path.
The rhythm in one's subconscious,
The melody of nature.
An undisclosed tristful fable,
A story of one and the millions.

Poetry.
An ecstatic connection,
Of myriad lives,
Fused in one verse,
Eternally.

//Mr. Might//

Far in the woods,
She lit a light.

The darkness vanished,
So did fright.

She was all alone there,
Until she crossed paths with a brave hunter called Mr.
Might.

Mr. Might asked her what was she doing all alone in the
dense forest.
She answered she was savoring the beautiful night.

The gentleman asked, "What's so beautiful about it?"
She replied, "The stars, the moon & you Mr. Might."

The man was shocked, his eyes popped out.
She just smiled and vanished mysteriously in the light.

//Apparition//

She had a peculiar feeling in her heart for him.
He was an apparition to her.
Beyond description.
Beyond knowledge.

He seemed unnatural.

But nature.
It is womb to queer things.
He wasn't a ghost.
He didn't scare her.
Just someone you rarely come across.

And she would have died a thousand deaths altogether,
If he ever left.

//The age of adage//

And once in a blue moon,
I am not afraid to shed a tear or two.
Some days deserve
To be full of clichés.
Just because some days are ordinary,
Does not mean you need to feel it too.

//Everyday phantasm//

The existence of ghosts is questionable.
Science denies it.
Stories support it.
I believe ghosts are for real,
In a world of art and imagination.

Where you feel somebody deceased around you,
It's your heart pouncing to be with them.

Ghosts are memories for me.

Good or bad but memories.

//A delightful dream//

She wanted him to sleep by her side
Every time she enclasped slumber,
She clutched his hand and
Pulled him along.

He never argued.
Never detested.
Always moved closer to her.
Hand in hand.

But they never woke up together.

She was his peace,
During the night-tide.

She was his illusion.
A thin air.
A beautiful dream.

//This churlish puzzle//

I cloistered myself behind the walls of illusion,
Confined me in my own imaginary world,
Magic secluded me from reality,
And I escaped the bitterness of truth,
My baleful fate was relieved from the demons of actuality.
I was relieved from life.

//When She paid me a visit//

That voice,
Had the power to elapse my sleep
I feel my almighty herself
entered my jaded life
That voice
Made be uncontrollable
I dance in the euphoria all the time
I wouldn't label it with any name
But just marvel at it.
She extended a friendly hand towards me
How can I not accept it?

//Her//

Every person
Garners a distinguished experience
Diverse from others

Every person
Creates their own philosophy
A unique life for themselves

Every person
Tries to impose their reality
Forgetting one's individuality

Every person
Believes in their superiority
That is why commotion exists

Every person
Needs a little love
To understand the absolute truth

Her.

//Tread on the land of joy//

Tread, Oh! Dire being.
On the land of joy,
Drink the nectar of contentment,
Dance on the tunes of cosmos.
This isn't a place for hatred,
The dubious have no place,
Anger has no face.
The god himself preaches a language here.

The language of acceptance.

//Patience//

I waited for the good things to happen,
I waited for the bad memories to wash away.

I waited for love,
To heal my wounds.

I waited for light,
To cease the darkness in me.

I waited for freedom,
From jaws of the devil.

I waited for god,
To rescue me from my fears.

I waited for peace,
For mending my heart.

I waited for myself,
To return back to my senses.

I waited.
I waited patiently.

It Paid me a visit
And I knew,
My search ends.

Patience.
That's all we need.
All our lives.

//Let's not suffer again//

I swallowed all the pain of this world.
I closed my eyes and looked into my hollow soul.
It suddenly brimmed with ecstasy.
The God rejoiced in our union.
In exchange, he took away all the pain from this earth.
No man would ever suffer again.
[Not willingly at least.]

//A prayer//

We are skin and bones outside,
Inside, we are what you are,
We are made up of you.
Then why are we so lost?
The realization of you,
To carry you in my heart,
Is the absolute delight.
To find you, in me,
Is a journey in itself.
The route is unknown.
Hurdles are countless.
Give me strength and understanding,
To find the right path
To walk towards you
To be joyous forever.
To be yours.

//Note to Self on having faith//

Beneath the sun
I open my diary
Let the rays illuminate my words
Write a note to me
That no matter what
I believe.
I believe in the power of bliss.
I believe in myself.
I believe in time.
I believe in holy chants of the river.
I believe in the sky holding mammoth knowledge.
I believe in discovering myself for my own good.
I believe in reinventing myself for everybody's good.
I believe in my own beauty.
I believe the words I am writing.
And, with these words, we will heal.
Scarred souls.
Make them believe.
Believe the wisdom.
Believe in the journey.
Believe Love & Life.
This powerful piece of paper,
Will never let you forget who you are,
Who I am,
Who we are.

//Power//

One fine day,
When the sun was in deep slumber,
And the wind's wrath stormed every shadow.
She took a flight,
She dived off into the wrecked sky,
without any fear,
without any angelic wings.
No one was present to hold her,
Someone who wouldn't let her fall.
But, she was sure that she'll fly,
She was free from all her terrors,
She believed in a mysterious power.
Maybe it was merely,
The power of love.
The power of joy.
The power of the system.
The power of her own soul.

//fear//

I wake up with a new fear every day,
A fear running in the back of my mind,
A fear captured in the veins of my heart,
Knowingly or Unknowingly,
fear resides wherever I go.
fear to end up my day like every other day.
I fear to hurt people without any such endeavors.
I fear getting mutilated too.
I fear the injuries.
I fear the uncertainties.
I fear the dark.
I fear the light.
I fear hatred.
I fear love.
I fear all bad.
I fear all good.
I fear the monsters, the witches, and the DEVIL.
I fear the humans, the animals, and the god.
I fear everything I'm living with.
I fear everything I'm living for.
I fear death.
I fear life.
Perhaps I also fear the 'BEYOND.'
I fear myself.
I fear my shadow.

I fear my demeanor.
I fear my soul.
But,
If I fear everything, then what am I alive for?
Did my creator weave me to fear all?
Is fear my destiny?
Will my days ever change?
Can I ever combat fear?
Take a carefree flight brimming with joy?
Fright is a perpetual foe.
We have to move our prospects afar from fear

Otherwise, we shall always remain enclosed.

Enclosed in a box.

A box of illusion.

Away from sanity.
Away from rationality.
Away from spirituality.
Away from independence.

We all shall live in a box of infinite fears.

//A quest to rediscover//

I am a wanderer,
I have a heart of a pirate.

I walk streets alone,
sail in typhoon, fly when it rains.

The world is beneath my feet,
I am born to conquer the universe.

While singing serenades of light,
I want to set on a journey.
A promenade to heaven,
Never return to this beautiful abode.
After all,
Beauty is such a materialistic word.

This place is one of its kind,
A different material altogether.
I'll remember all the signboards.
All the food joints.
And all the temples.

I'll create my own world in my body.
Assimilate the earth in me,
And be an unforgettable molecule of the universe.

The Promenade

I am a vagabond,
On a quest,
To discover who I am.

Life is a tough voyage,
Full of dejections,
Thorns laid on every road I walk,
An impossible expedition,
Never satisfies you till the end.
Is it life, or us being hard?

Life is still a journey,
A quest,
But whether it is miserable or not?
It's up to the traveler to decide.

//No Phoenix, No Dragon//

There's fire in his heart
Ready to take flight
Into a different world
Where there's no plight

He slowly takes off
Rises up in the air
He never knew it before
To fly with such flair

People who knew him were stunned
His actions were protested against
Amidst this turmoil
Nobody understood his angst

He was watching the world turning grey
Above from the sky
People preparing for battle
For their kings, malicious and sly

Monarchs know his miracles
They wished they knew prophets
Who manifested his existence in oracles.

The Promenade

He flew free in the air
Unlike Phoenix and Dragons
With eyes and heart sealed with fire

The universe above him
Was for him to explore
The poetry he thought of
Turned out to be a silent roar

Little children tried hard to
Chase his shadow on the ground
Enraged parents pulled them into houses
Cursing him with words twisted

He approached him with a sudden swift

People saw his shadow fading away
He was going farther
They realized he meant no harm

He existed just to spread the words of morality.

He splashed the water of peace with his fiery wings
The entire cosmos

Was enlightened with the wisdom of life
Putting end to all existing riddles

People will always cherish him
Kings will despise him
And he,
Will live on forever.

//We are the Universe//

i
We need to come together urgently.
Together in flesh and soul.
Reside together in one sacred space,
Hold each other's hands,
And feel the glory,
Bestowed upon us.
There's a message for all of us.
It's a dream we all see with our eyes closed.

ii
Every moment, she makes manifestations of love.
A love, as real as the Sun.
Do not misconstrue love with mere mirage's.
We are on a mission to decode that love.
To spread the word, as soon as we realize it.
We are all attached to an umbilical cord.
A cord that holds the universe together.

iii
You and I, don't know each other,
 Yet, we do.
We have met before
And we will keep meeting eternally.
That's how the cosmos works.
We expand with joy.
We have created infinite spirals.

We know it all.
After all,
We are the Universe.

Note of Gratitude

This is my first book ever and I want to use this rare opportunity to thank my mother. She lived a short and discontented life due to her illness, but had some lively dreams. She dedicated those dreams to us, my brother and I. She was aware of the fact that she wouldn't be around, to watch us grow become fuller humans but she had a clear idea of what we'll become. She knew she nurtured artists in her house. Although she emphasized on our academics during the daylight, she whispered poetry in our ears by night. She cast this inescapable spell on me with her poems and stories that it shaped my entire existence. Hindu Mythology constitutes 'The Holy Trinity', Brahma, Vishnu and Mahesh. My mother was my Brahma, for she birthed me. My Mithamaa, my youngest aunt was my Mahesh, for she destroyed my ignorance and felicity to give me an honest perspective of life. My Kuttymaa, my older aunt, continues to foster me with strength in this deceitful world.

I wrote the third chapters, 'The Salty Ocean' when I longed for my mother, when I longed for love. But it was after my Mithamaa's demise, I followed that chapter with 'The Magic Unravels', when I truly fell in love with the. I know my reaction should've been the opposite but it was her death that brought me closer to everything in this world. It sensitized me. It was a reminder that the life is short, but it eventually moves on. Life did move on with their memories fueling my pen. When the two pillars holding me collapsed without any traces, the pillars multiplied.

I love you all for keeping me grounded, I am certain I have forgotten a lot of names, you know how the stress of writing an acknowledgement is, so please forgive me and remember my love for you.

Thank You.